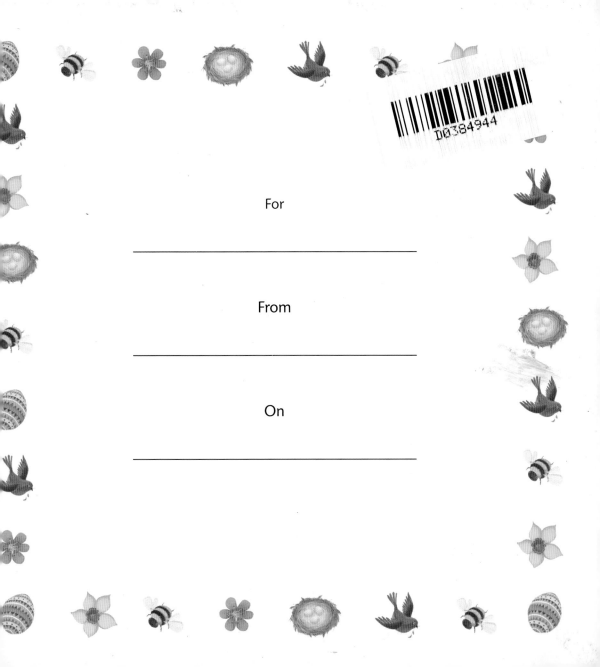

For

_____

From

_____

On

_____

To the Wells Family—who celebrate Jesus every day. —C.B.

To David and Laura —R.J.

ZONDERKIDZ

Lily's Easter Party
Copyright © 2013 by Zondervan
Illustrations © 2013 by Richard Johnson

Published in partnership with FamilyLife®.

Requests for information should be addressed to:

Zonderkidz, 5300 Patterson Ave SE, Grand Rapids, Michigan 49530

Library of Congress Cataloging-in-Publication Data
Bowman, Crystal.
    Lily's Easter party / by Crystal Bowman.
        p. cm.
    Summary: Lily, her brother, and some friends go on a special, surprise Easter egg hunt that reveals the story of Jesus's death and resurrection. Includes activities.
    ISBN 978-0-310-72595-4
    [1. Easter—Fiction. 2. Jesus Christ—Passion—Fiction. 3. Parties—Fiction. 4. Christian life—Fiction.] I. Title.
    PZ.B6834Lhm 2013
    [E]-dc23   2012030270

Editor: Mary Hassinger
Art direction & design: Jody Langley

Printed in China

12 13 14 15 16 17 /LPC/ 6 5 4 3 2 1

Lily's Easter Party

The Story of the Resurrection Eggs®

By Crystal Bowman
Illustrated by Richard Johnson

FAMILYLIFE®

ZONDERkidz

ZONDERVAN.com/
AUTHORTRACKER
follow your favorite authors

How to use this book

Lily's Easter Surprise is a special story about a young girl and her friends learning about God's great love for us. Lily's parents share their faith with Lily and her friends using a unique and "super secret" egg hunt.

By sharing Lily's story with the children in your life, you are giving them a great and wonderful gift … the true story of Easter in a way that children can understand and remember. By including the sharing of the scripture references under each illustration on the next page, you are showing your child the power of God's Word.

Suggested activities

1. Set up an egg hunt for your children, neighborhood, or a small Sunday school group. Follow the example of Lily's parents and run your hunt in a similar way.

2. Read the story in a group setting and then have a hunt for the eggs. Bring the children back and have them tell about each egg that they found, revealing the symbol inside each one.

3. For a complete set of Resurrection Eggs® to use for your egg hunt go to www.shopFamilyLife.com or visit your local Christian bookstore.

Explanation of Resurrection Eggs

Blue Egg
Little Donkey
Read Matthew 21:1–11

Light Pink Egg
Silver Coins
Read Matthew 26:14–16

Light Purple Egg
Cup
*Read Matthew
26:17–19, 26–28*

Orange Egg
Praying Hands
Read Mark 14:32–40

Green Egg
Leather Whip
Read John 18:28–19:1

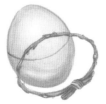

Yellow Egg
Crown of Thorns
Read Matthew 27:27–31

Light Orange Egg
Nails in the Cross
Read John 19:16–18

Light Green Egg
A Die
Read John 19:23–24

Purple Egg
Spear
Read John 19:31–37

Light Blue Egg
White Linen Cloth
*Read Matthew
27: 57–60*

Pink Egg
Stone
Read Matthew 28:1–4

White Egg
Empty
Read Matthew 28: 1–8

"I'm going to find a whole bunch of Easter eggs this year," said Lily. "But I'll let Lucas find some too."

Mom smiled. "I'm happy you're going to let Lucas find some of the eggs," she said. "Our Easter egg hunt is going to be extra super special this year."

Lily's eyes got as big as Easter eggs. "For real?" she said.

"Yes—for real," said Mom. "It's a secret surprise. You'll have to wait until Saturday to find out."

Lily loved surprises. But it was very hard for her to wait.

Lily rode her bike down the sidewalk. She saw Isabelle drawing chalk pictures. "Hey, Isabelle!" said Lily. "Guess what? Our Easter egg hunt is going to be extra super special. It's a secret surprise. Do you want to come?"

"Yes!" said Isabelle.

"Good," Lily said. "Come to my house on Saturday at one o'clock and meet me in the backyard."

"Okay," said Isabelle. "See you then."

Lily kept riding. She saw Maria playing with her dolls. "Hi, Maria!" said Lily. "Guess what? Our Easter egg hunt is going to be extra super special. It's a secret surprise. Do you want to come?"

"Yes!" said Maria.

"Good," said Lily. "Come to my house on Saturday at one o'clock. Isabelle is coming too."

"Okay," said Maria. "I will come."

Lily rode her bike a little farther. She saw Noah and James playing catch in the park. "Hey, guys!" she said. "Our Easter egg hunt is going to be extra super special. It's a secret surprise! Do you want to come?"

"Yes!" said Noah and James together.

"Good," said Lily. "Come to my house on Saturday at one o'clock and meet me in the backyard. Isabelle and Maria are coming too."

Lily rode her bike home. She went inside for a snack. "I asked my friends to come to our extra super special Easter egg hunt," she told Mom as she chewed her apple slices.

"Good!" Mom said. "They will like the secret surprise."

"Me too," said Lucas as he clapped his hands.

Lily laughed at Lucas. "You're silly," she said. "It's a good thing you don't know what the surprise is! You would tell everyone. Sometimes little brothers aren't very good at keeping secrets."

"By Saturday afternoon, you will find out the secret surprise," said Mom. "And you and Lucas can share the surprise with your friends."

Lily let out a big sigh. "I can hardly wait!" she said.

On Saturday morning, while Lily and Lucas were still asleep, Mom and Dad snuck into the backyard and carefully hid Easter eggs. They tucked one egg under a small pile of leaves. They hid another egg in the rose bushes and covered another with some small stones. They placed one egg next to the garden hose and buried a special egg in the sandbox. Soon all of the eggs were hidden.

At one o'clock, everyone met in the backyard.

"Everyone is here," Lily said. "Can we start?"

"It's almost time," said Dad. "Now everyone listen. There are twelve eggs hidden in the backyard. Be careful not to step on them. When you find one, put it in the basket on the picnic table. Then you may look for another egg. Do not open any of them until we have all twelve eggs. Do you understand?"

"YES!" the children all said together.

"Me too!" said Lucas.

Dad said, "Get ready. Get set. Go!"

The children searched everywhere.

"I found a purple egg!" Maria said.

"I found a green egg!" hollered Noah.

Lily found an orange egg, James a light blue one, and Isabelle a bright pink one. They brought their eggs to the basket and went to search for more.

When no one was watching the basket, Lucas reached in and pulled out the green egg. He ran and hid it behind the big tree. "I hid an egg!" he said.

"Oh no, Lucas!" Dad said as everyone giggled. "You don't have to hide the eggs again. Let's keep them in the basket."

Lucas put the green egg back. Then Lily helped him find a blue egg.

He ran to the picnic table and placed it in the basket.

"Good job, Lucas!" said Lily. Let's find another one."

When the basket was almost full, they counted the eggs together. One, two, three, four, five, six, seven, eight, nine, ten, eleven.

"We're missing one," Lily said.

"It's the special one," said Dad. "Let's go to the sandbox and look for it together."

Everyone started digging. Sand went flying everywhere. The children dug through the sand until Lucas squealed with delight.

"I found it! I found it!" Lucas said as he held up a white egg.

"Yea for Lucas!" everyone cheered.

"And now it's time for our secret surprise," said Mom.

Lily and her friends sat around the picnic table. Then Mom took out the blue egg and gave it to Noah.

"Go ahead, Noah. Open the egg."

Noah carefully opened the egg. He reached into the egg and took out a little brown donkey. "What's this for?" he asked.

Mom explained. "When Jesus lived on earth, many people thought he was going to be their new king. One day, as Jesus rode into town on a donkey, people waved palm branches and cheered, 'Blessed is he who comes in the name of the Lord! Hosanna in the highest!'

Everyone wanted to see Jesus as he rode by on the donkey."

    Dad took a light pink egg from the basket and gave it to Isabelle. She opened the egg and found three silver coins. "Do you know what the coins are for?" Dad asked.

    "To buy something?" said Isabelle.

    "That's a good guess," said Dad. "Here's the story. Jesus had a lot of friends, but not everyone was his friend. Some people wanted to kill Jesus, and they needed one of his friends to help them. Judas Iscariot was one of Jesus' friends who turned against him. The people who wanted to kill Jesus gave Judas thirty silver coins to help them find Jesus. Judas loved money more than he loved Jesus. That's what the coins are for."

"Let's open another egg," Mom said. She picked the light purple egg and gave it to Lily.

"It's a cup," Lily said. "Did they have something to drink?"

"Yes, they did," said Mom. "Jesus' closest friends were called disciples. Jesus told his disciples to prepare a special dinner. While they ate their dinner that night, Jesus poured wine into a cup and told them to drink it. He told them the wine was like his blood, and that it would help them to remember what Jesus was about to do. He also shared some bread with them and told them the bread was like his body. The disciples didn't understand what Jesus meant until later."

Dad picked the orange egg out of the basket and gave it to James. James opened the egg.

"It looks like two hands that are praying," he said.

"That's right, James," Dad said. "After the special dinner Jesus ate with his disciples, they went to a garden to pray. Jesus asked his disciples to pray for him while he went to talk to God by himself. While Jesus prayed, his disciples fell asleep. But Jesus kept on praying. He knew he was going to die. He knew it was going to be very hard. That's why he prayed that night. He prayed for God's will to be done."

Mom took the green egg from the basket and gave it to Maria.

Maria opened the egg and took out a strip of leather. "What does this mean?" she asked.

Mom said, "Some soldiers who wanted to kill Jesus found him in the garden where he had been praying. They arrested him and took him to their ruler, Pilate. Pilate asked Jesus a lot of questions. Even though Jesus had not done anything wrong, Pilate told the soldiers to whip him. They whipped Jesus with leather whips until he started to bleed."

"That's really sad," said Maria.

"Yes, it is," said Mom.

Then Mom gave Lucas the yellow egg. Lucas pulled the egg
apart and took out a circle.

"What's this?" he said.

"If you look at it closely, it looks like small branches twisted

together," said Mom. "The soldiers who whipped Jesus took some branches with thorns and
made a crown to put on Jesus' head. They laughed at him and shouted, 'Hail! King of the Jews!'
The soldiers did this to make fun of Jesus because he said he was a king. It was just another
way they were being mean to Jesus."

"We have more eggs to open," Dad said. He gave the light orange egg to Noah.

"It's a cross," he said.

"What is it made from?" asked Dad.

"It looks like nails," Noah said.

"That's exactly what they are," said Dad. "Long ago, people who committed crimes—like robbers and murderers—were put to death by being nailed to a cross. That's what they did to Jesus. He hung on a cross in between two robbers who were also on crosses."

"But Jesus hadn't done anything wrong," Noah said. "So why did he have to die?"

"It's part of God's plan for us," said Dad. "We don't always do the right thing. Sometimes we sin and disobey God. But because God loves us so much, he wants to forgive us. Jesus died on the cross so that all who believe in him can have their sins forgiven."

Mom picked the light green egg from the basket and gave it to Isabelle to open.

"It's a die," said Isabelle. "Did the soldiers play a game?"

"Not the kind of games that we play with dice," said Mom. "The soldiers were very greedy. They probably thought Jesus' clothes would be worth a lot of money. They divided his clothes into four parts, but didn't want to tear his garment, so they played a game—sort of like rolling dice—to see who would get the robe. The die reminds us again of how mean some of the people were. But Jesus died for them too."

"Next we need to open the purple egg. Go ahead, Lily," Dad said.

Lily opened the purple egg and took out a little spear. "That looks sharp!" she said. "What did they use it for?"

"It's a very sad part of the story," said Dad. "The soldiers were in a hurry to take the bodies off the crosses because the next day was the Sabbath. So to make sure the men would die soon, they broke their legs. When the soldiers came to Jesus, they saw he had already died, so they didn't break his legs. They pierced his side with the spear instead. In the Old Testament it says that not one of Jesus' bones would be broken. And that's exactly what happened."

30

Mom took two eggs out of the basket. She gave one to James and one to Maria. "What's in the light blue egg, James?" Mom asked.

"It's a white piece of cloth," he said as he opened the egg.

"It's called linen," said Mom. "In Bible times they used large pieces of linen to wrap around the body of someone who had died. Then they would put the body in a tomb which is like a cave. A rich man, named Joseph, asked for Jesus' body, and Pilate agreed. Joseph wrapped Jesus' body in a clean linen cloth and placed it in a tomb.

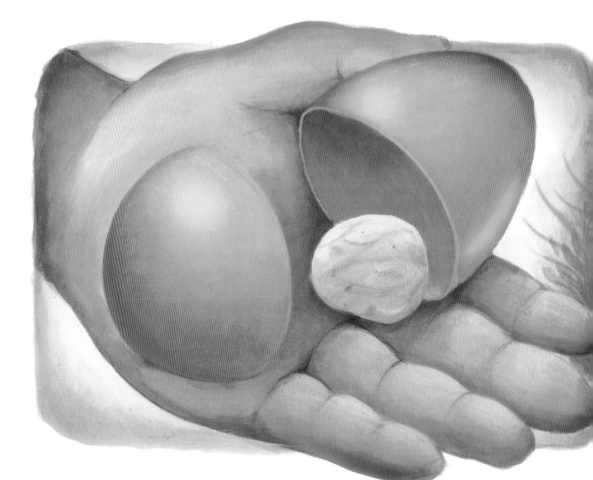

"Maria, you can open the pink egg."

"It's a stone," Maria said.

Mom continued the story. "After Joseph put Jesus' body in the tomb, he rolled a big, heavy stone in front of the tomb as some of Jesus' friends watched. Then they all walked away. They were very sad. They thought they would never see Jesus again."

"We have one egg left," Dad said. "It's the special white one that Lucas found in the sandbox."

He gave it to Lucas to open. But when Lucas pulled the egg apart, there was nothing inside! Lucas shook it up and down, but nothing came out.

"It's empty!" Lily said. "Why isn't there anything inside?"

"This is the best part of the story," said Dad. "Early Sunday morning, two women who were close friends of Jesus, decided to go to his tomb. There was a great earthquake, and an angel of the Lord came down from heaven and rolled the stone away from the tomb. When they got there, the women looked in the tomb. Jesus' body was not there! The angel said to the women, 'Don't be afraid. Jesus is not here—he has risen from the dead! Go into Galilee and you will see him there.'

"The women were so excited! They ran to tell Jesus' friends, but on the way they saw Jesus himself! It was true! Jesus had risen from the dead!"

"And then what?" asked Lily.

"Then Jesus appeared to many of his friends and disciples. They were so happy to see him. But Jesus didn't stay on earth much longer because his work on earth was finished. Jesus went up to heaven, and that is where he is today. Because Jesus died on the cross and rose again, everyone who believes in him will live with him forever."

"This was the best egg hunt ever!" said Lily.

Then she had an idea. Lily invited all of her friends to come to church with her on Easter Sunday.

And they all said YES!